3 4028 07622 4352
HARRIS COUNTY PUBLIC LIBRARY

J 970.3 Kis
Kissock, Heather
Apache

DISCARD

$17.99
ocn519835209
01/03/2011

W9-AMN-116

American Indian Art and Culture

APACHE

**Heather Kissock and
Jordan McGill**

WEIGL PUBLISHERS INC.
"Creating Inspired Learning"
www.weigl.com

Published by Weigl Publishers Inc.
350 5th Avenue, 59th Floor
New York, NY 10118

Website: www.weigl.com

Copyright ©2011 Weigl Publishers Inc.
All rights reserved. No part of this publication may be reproduced, stored in a retrieval system, or transmitted in any form or by
any means, electronic, mechanical, photocopying, recording, or otherwise, without the prior written permission of the publisher.

Library of Congress Cataloging-in-Publication Data

Kissock, Heather.
 Apache : American Indian art and culture / Heather Kissock and Jordan McGill.
    p. cm.
 Includes index.
 ISBN 978-1-60596-991-6 (hardcover : alk. paper) -- ISBN 978-1-60596-992-3 (softcover : alk. paper) -- ISBN 978-1-60596-993-0 (e-book)
 1. Apache art--Juvenile literature. 2. Apache Indians--Material culture--Juvenile literature. 3. Apache Indians--Social life and customs--Juvenile
literature. I. McGill, Jordan. II. Title.
 E99.A6K57 2010
 970.004'97--dc22
                        2010005331

Printed in the United States of America in North Mankato, Minnesota
1 2 3 4 5 6 7 8 9 0 14 13 12 11 10

042010
WEP264000

Photograph and Text Credits
Cover: Courtesy, National Museum of the American Indian, Smithsonian Institution (13/3936); Alamy: pages 4, 7, 14, 15, 16, 17, 20; Getty Images: pages 5,
6, 10, 11, 22, 23; Courtesy, National Museum of the American Indian, Smithsonian Institution: pages 8L (2/1279), 9T (13/3936), 9M (12/3380), 9B
(23/4014), 13 (10/5453); Nativestock: pages 8T, 12, 21.

Every reasonable effort has been made to trace ownership and to obtain permission to reprint copyright material. The publishers would be pleased to have
any errors or omissions brought to their attention so that they may be corrected in subsequent printings.

All of the Internet URLs given in the book were valid at the time of publication. However, due to the dynamic nature of the Internet, some addresses may
have changed, or sites may have ceased to exist since publication. While the author and publisher regret any inconvenience this may cause readers, no
responsibility for any such changes can be accepted by either the author or the publisher.

PROJECT COORDINATOR   Heather Kissock

DESIGN   Terry Paulhus

ILLUSTRATOR   Martha Jablonski-Jones

Contents

The People

The Apache are a group of American Indians that **traditionally** lived in the mountains and plains of Texas, Oklahoma, New Mexico, and Arizona. They moved to these areas in the 1500s from what is now Canada.

The Apache are made up of six separate tribes. These are the Western Apache, Chiricahua, Mescalero, Jicarillo, Lipan, and Kiowa. In the past, each tribe had its own land.

Today, there are about 55,000 Apache in the United States. Most live on **reservations** in New Mexico, Arizona, and Oklahoma.

NET LINK

Find out what the Apache call themselves and what it means at **www.mnsu.edu/emuseum/ cultural/northamerica/apache.html**.

Apache Homes

WICKIUPS In the past, the Apache lived in wickiups. A wickiup was a dome-shaped house. It was made of tall **saplings** that were bent and pushed into the ground to make a frame. Tree bark or woven rushes were laid over the frame to make the walls.

Apache Ideas

The hides at the bottom of the teepee could be rolled up in hot weather to allow a breeze to enter.

TEEPEES

When the Apache went hunting, they lived in teepees. These cone-shaped tents were made of long poles and animal skins. Teepees were easy to put up and take down. This helped the Apache move quickly when they were following animal herds.

Apache Clothing

BUCKSKIN CLOTHING

In the past, women wore buckskin dresses, and men wore leather shirts and breechcloths. These were small strips of material that covered the body below the waist. Later, both men and women began to wear clothing made from cotton.

JEWELRY

Traditionally, the Apache used shells, wood, and parts of animals to make beads for necklaces and other jewelry. After Europeans arrived in the area, the Apache began using glass beads.

HEADWEAR

Most Apache men wore wide headbands to keep sweat out of their eyes. Some men wore deerskin caps instead.

DECORATION

The Apache often decorated their clothing. They would add fringes and beading to their dresses and shirts.

MOCCASINS

The Apache wore moccasins on their feet. These slipper-like shoes were made from soft leather. Some Apache wore boots made from leather as well.

Hunting and Gathering

AGAVE

Agave was a **staple** of the Apache diet. The plant was roasted for days before it was eaten.

BERRIES

Women picked a variety of berries. These were eaten fresh or dried for later use.

BISON

Bison was the Apache's main meat source. The meat could be roasted, boiled, eaten raw, or dried for later use.

Most Apache hunted their food when they first moved to the southern United States. Other Apache farmed the land and grew their own food. When the crops were **harvested**, they would begin to hunt as well.

CORN

Corn was a major part of the Apache diet. It was eaten on its own or put in breads.

SAP

Sap from box elder trees was mixed with shavings from the inside of animal hides. This made a sweet candy.

ACORNS

The Apache ate the acorns of gambel oaks. Tea was made from the tree's bark.

Apache Tools

BOWS AND ARROWS

The Apache used materials from nature to make many tools. Bows and arrows were made from wood. Rock was chipped down to make arrowheads. The bow's string was made from animal **sinew**.

Apache Idea

To store water, the Apache would basket with **pinon gum**. This ma basket waterproof.

SHIELDS

The Apache carried shields to protect themselves from enemies. The shields were made from bison hide. They were often and decorated with **sacred** objects.

Moving from Place to Place

WALKING

In the past, the Apache walked from place to place, even when traveling long distances. Once Europeans brought horses to North America, the Apache quickly started to rely on horses for transportation.

Apache Ideas

Horses could pull more weight than dogs, so the Apache began building bigger teepees. Some were up to 24 feet high. When dogs pulled travois, the teepees were about half that size.

TRAVOIS

When walking, the Apache used travois to move their goods from place to place. A travois is a type of sled. At first, dogs were used to pull travois. Later, the Apache used horses.

Apache Music and Dance

DANCE

Dancing played an important role in Apache life. Dances were performed in honor of important events. Some Apache girls performed the sunrise dance. This dance signaled the passage into adulthood. It also prepared the girl for a long and healthy life.

Singing and drumming played an important role in Apache ceremonies. **Shamans** sang and drummed to protect and heal people.

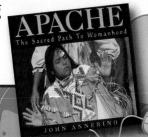

APACHE
The Sacred Path To Womanhood

JOHN ANNERINO

NET LINK
Learn more about the sunrise dance at **www.webwinds.com/yupanqui/ apachesunrise.htm**.

Why Bat Hangs Upside Down

One day, Coyote decided that it was time to find a wife. He did not know who his wife should be, so he asked Bat for help. Bat remembered that Hawk had disappeared a while ago, leaving his wife behind. He suggested that Coyote take Hawk's wife as his own.

Coyote thought this would be a good idea, but Hawk returned and learned of the plan. He became angry at Bat for giving Coyote this idea.

Hawk went to Bat and grabbed him. Lifting Bat from the ground, Hawk tossed him into some nearby bushes. Bat landed upside down in the bush, grasping its branches. From this day on, bats have been known to hang upside down, even when they are sleeping.

Apache Art

BASKETS

Apache women were known as skilled basket makers. They wove baskets out of willow branches. Large baskets called granaries were used to store grain and vegetables.

POTTERY

Apache pottery was used to carry and store items. The pots were often painted with patterns and symbols that were important to the Apache.

NET LINK

Read more about other Apache crafts at **www.ehow.com/about_4566318_apache-arts-crafts.html**.

Apache Wojape

Ingredients

A big bowl of berries (fresh
or frozen)
1 cup corn syrup or 2 cups
white sugar
1 tablespoon cornstarch
Water

Instructions

1. Mash the berries in the bottom of a large, flat-bottomed pot.
2. Add the water and syrup.
3. With an adult's help, place the pot on the stove, and bring the mixture
   to a boil. Let it simmer for 15 to 20 minutes.
4. Dissolve the cornstarch in cold water, and add to the mixture until it
   reaches the desired thickness.
5. Remove the pot from the stove, and pour the treat into serving bowls.
6. Serve warm, and enjoy!

Glossary

harvested: gathered a crop

pinon gum: a sticky material found on pinon pine trees

reservations: land set aside by the government for American Indians

sacred: religious

saplings: young trees

shamans: people who heal others

sinew: a strong cord that joins a muscle to a bone

staple: a product that everyone needs or uses

traditionally: related to beliefs, practices, and objects that have been passed down from one generation to the next

Index